HYMNS
YOU LOVE
40 Timeless Hymns from Yesterday & Today

Shawnee Press, Inc.

A Subsidiary of Music Sales Corporation
1221 17th Avenue South · Nashville, TN 37212

Visit Shawnee Press Online at
www.shawneepress.com

SB1017

HYMNS
YOU LOVE
40 Timeless Hymns from Yesterday & Today

How Great Thou Art

Stuart K. Hine

Swedish Folk melody
Adapted by Stuart K. Hine

Verse 3

And when I think that God, His Son not sparing,
Sent Him to die— I scarce can take it in:
That on the Cross, my burden gladly bearing,
He bled and died to take away my sin:

Verse 4

When Christ shall come with shout of acclamation
And take me home, what joy shall fill my heart!
Then I shall bow in humble adoration,
And there proclaim, my God, how great Thou art!

Great Is Thy Faithfulness

Thomas O. Chisholm

William M. Runyan

Verse 3
Pardon for sin and a peace that endureth
Thine own dear presence to cheer and to guide;
Strength for today and bright hope for tomorrow,
Blessings all mine, with ten thousand beside!

The Old Rugged Cross

George Bennard   George Bennard

Verse 3

In the old rugged cross, stained with blood so divine,
A wondrous beauty I see;
For 'twas on that old cross Jesus suffered and died
To pardon and sanctify me.

Verse 4

To the old rugged cross I will ever be true;
It's shame and reproach gladly bear.
Then He'll call me some day to my home far away,
Where His glory forever I'll share.

Morning Has Broken

Eleanor Farjeon

Traditional Gaelic melody

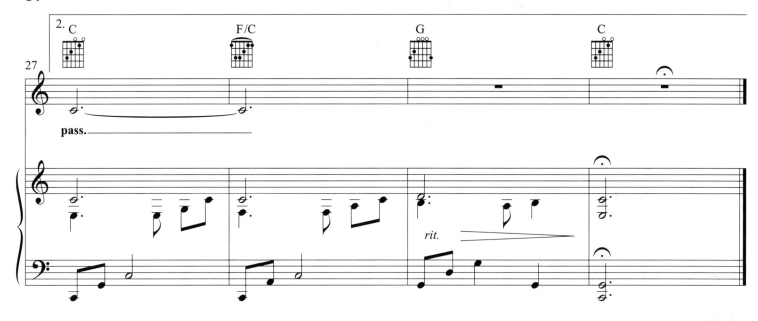

Verse 3

Mine is the sunlight!
Mine is the morning
Born of the one light
Eden saw play!

Praise with elation,
Praise ev'ry morning,
God's recreation
Of the new day!

Because He Lives

William J. and Gloria Gaither

William J. Gaither

16

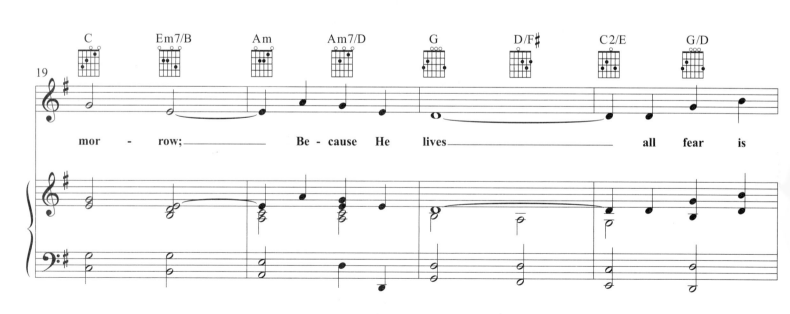

Verse 3
And then one day I'll cross that river,
I'll fight life's final war with pain;
And then as death gives way to vict'ry,
I'll see the lights of glory and I'll know He reigns.

In Christ Alone

Keith Getty and Stuart Townend

Keith Getty and Stuart Townend

19

His Name Is Wonderful

Audrey Mieir

Audrey Mieir

Glorify Thy Name

Donna Adkins   **Donna Adkins**

There's Something About That Name

William J. Gaither and Gloria Gaither

William J. Gaither

My Tribute
(To God Be the Glory)

Andraé Crouch

Andraé Crouch

Why Do I Sing About Jesus?

Albert A. Ketchum

Albert A. Ketchum

Verse 3
He is the Fairest of fair ones;
He is the Lily, the Rose.
Rivers of mercy surround Him;
Grace, love and pity He shows.

We Have Come into His House

Bruce Ballinger

Bruce Ballinger

33

Thou Art Worthy

Pauline M. Mills

Pauline M. Mills

Heaven Came Down

John W. Peterson

John W. Peterson

Verse 3

Now I've a hope that will surely endure after the passing of time;
I have a future in heaven for sure there in those mansions sublime.
And it's because of that wonderful day, when at the cross I believed;
Riches eternal and blessings supernal, from His precious hand I received.

Majesty

Jack Hayford

Jack Hayford

Spirit of the Living God

Daniel Iverson, stanza 1
Lowell Alexander, stanzas 2, 3

Daniel Iverson

Verse 3

Holy presence, love divine, cast out my fear.
Holy presence, love divine, cast out my fear.
Shield me, free me, call me, lead me.
Holy presence, love divine, cast out my fear.

Sweet, Sweet Spirit

Doris Akers

Doris Akers

45

I Want to Walk As a Child of the Light

Kathleen Thomerson

Kathleen Thomerson

star of my life_____ is the Je - sus.
show me the way to is the Fa - ther.

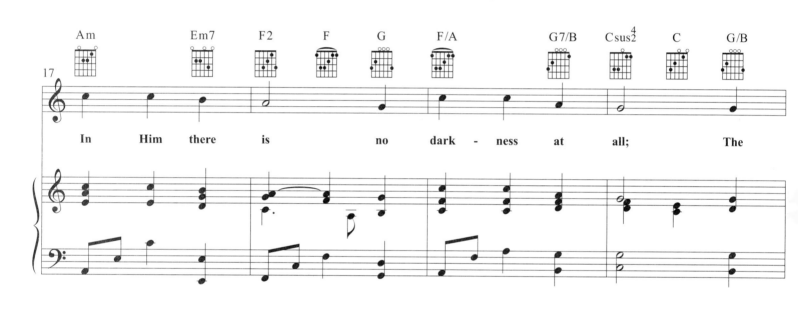

In Him there is no dark - ness at all; The

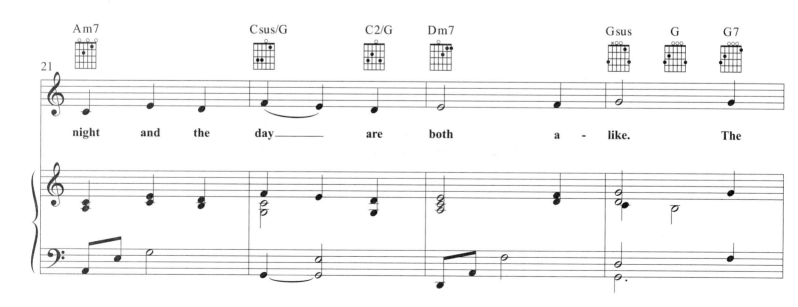

night and the day_____ are both a - like. The

Verse 3
I'm looking for the coming of Christ;
I want to be with Jesus.
When we have run with patience the race,
We shall know the joy of Jesus.

Holy Ground

Geron Davis

Geron Davis

Turn Your Eyes upon Jesus

Helen H. Lemmel

Helen H. Lemmel

Warmly ♩ = 92 - 96

Turn your eyes up-on Je - sus, Look full in His won-der-ful face, And the things of earth will grow strange - ly dim, In the light of His glo - ry and grace.

Love Lifted Me

James Rowe

Howard E. Smith

Verse 3

Souls in danger look above,
Jesus completely saves.
He will lift you by His love,
Out of the angry waves.

He's the Master of the sea,
Billows His will obey,
He your Saviour wants to be,
Be saved today.

Now I Belong to Jesus

Norman J. Clayton

Norman J. Clayton

Verse 3

**Joy floods my soul for Jesus has saved me,
Freed me from sin that long had enslaved me.
His precious blood, He came to redeem,
Now I belong to Him;**

It's So Wonderful

Ralph H. Good Pasteur

Ralph H. Good Pasteur

The Family of God

William J. and Gloria Gaither

William J. Gaither

Surely Goodness and Mercy

John W. Peterson and Alfred B. Smith
Based on Psalm 23

John W. Peterson and Alfred B. Smith

64

days, all the days of my life._____ All the

days, all the days of my life._____

Verse 3
When I walk through the dark, lonesome valley,
My Savior will walk with me there;
And safely His great hand will lead me
To the mansions He's gone to prepare.

Victory in Jesus

Eugene M. Bartlett, Sr.

Eugene M. Bartlett, Sr.

Verse 3

I heard about a mansion
He has built for me in glory,
And I heard about the streets of gold
Beyond the crystal sea;

About the angels singing,
And the old redemption story;
And some sweet day I'll sing up there
The song of victory.

The Longer I Serve Him

William J. Gaither   **William J. Gaither**

He Lives

Alfred H. Ackley

Alfred H. Ackley

A7   Am7/D   D   G

long life's nar - row way._____ He lives,_____ He lives_____ sal -

Am7   B7   E7

va - tion to im - part!_____ You ask me how I

A7   Am7/D   C/G   G

rit.

know He lives? He lives with - in my heart._____

rit.

Verse 3
Rejoice, rejoice, O Christians, lift up your voice and sing
Eternal hallelujahs to Jesus Christ the King!
The Hope of all who seek Him, the Help of all who find,
None other is so loving, so good and kind.

We Will Glorify

Twila Paris   **Twila Paris**

In the Garden

C. Austin Miles

C. Austin Miles

Verse 3

I'd stay in the garden with Him
Though the night around me be falling,
But He bids me go; through the voice of woe
His voice to me is calling.

He Touched Me

William J. Gaither

William J. Gaither

In His Time

Diane Ball

Diane Ball

Great Is the Lord

Michael W. Smith and Deborah D. Smith

Michael W. Smith and Deborah D. Smith

How Majestic Is Your Name

Michael W. Smith

Michael W. Smith

Lamb of God

Twila Paris

Twila Paris

I Will Call upon the Lord

Michael O'Shields
Based on Psalm 18:3; 2 Samuel 22:47

Michael O'Shields

Lively, march-like ♩ = 100

I will call up-on the Lord Who is wor-thy to be praised. So shall I be saved from my en-e-mies. I will call up-on the Lord. Lord. The

He Has Made Me Glad

(I Will Enter His Gates)

Leona Von Brethorst   Leona Von Brethorst

More Precious than Silver

Lynn DeShazo

Lynn DeShazo

Soon and Very Soon

Andraé Crouch

Andraé Crouch

Verse 3

No more dying there— we are going to see the King!
No more dying there— we are going to see the King!
No more dying there— we are going to see the King!
Hallelujah! Hallelujah! We're going to see the King!

I'll Fly Away

Albert E. Brumley

Albert E. Brumley

Verse 3
Just a few more weary days and then,
I'll fly away;
To a land where joys shall never end,
I'll fly away.

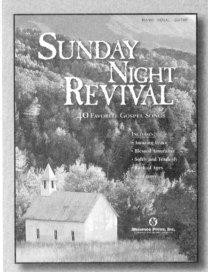
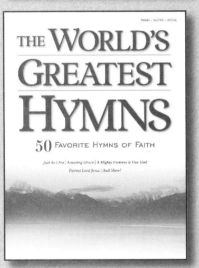
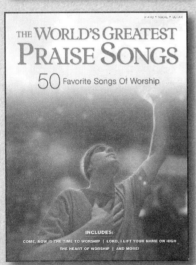
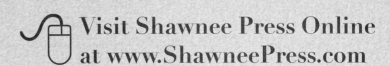